Growing up during
THE NORMAN CONQUEST

Frances Wilkins

B.T. Batsford Ltd *London*

First published 1980
Second impression 1984

ISBN 0 7134 3360 4

Printed and bound in Great Britain by
Anchor Brendon Ltd,
Tiptree, Essex
for the Publishers Batsford Academic and
Educational, an imprint of
B T Batsford Ltd,
4 Fitzhardinge Street, London W1H 0AH

Frontispiece **A doctor's pupil**

Acknowledgment

The Author and Publishers thank the following for their kind permission to reproduce copyright illustrations: the British Library for figs 21, 42, 43, 47, 49, 56, 61; the Trustees of the British Museum for figs 6, 18, 31, 54, 67, 69, 70; the British Tourist Authority for fig 40; the Courtauld Institute for figs 46, 68; Pat Hodgson Picture Library for figs 2, 60; A.F. Kersting for figs 10, 33; National Portrait Gallery for fig 37; Newcastle University Library for fig 57; Radio Times Hulton Picture Library for figs 3, 4, 5, 9, 14, 20, 22, 24, 25, 27, 28, 38, 39, 50, 51, 55, 58; R.J. Unstead for figs 19, 26 (from *Looking at History*, A & C Black Ltd, 1955). Thanks are expressed also to Pat Hodgson for the picture research on this book.

Contents

The Illustrations

1 The Normans

In 1066, at the Battle of Hastings, the Saxon King Harold of England was defeated by the Normans from France. Duke William of Normandy became King of England and the Norman conquerors settled down in this country. At that period the Normans were among the most able and advanced people in Europe, and their arrival in England altered the way of life of nearly the whole population.

One of the greatest influences the Normans had was in developing the feudal system. This was a form of government based entirely on landholdings, although its main aim was to provide the King with a loyal

1   The Norman invaders of England kill King Harold. William the Conqueror became King and during his reign England adopted Norman customs. This is part of the Bayeux Tapestry.

2 William the Conqueror, King of England, grants lands to his nephew, the Earl of Brittany.

3 A blacksmith and two other peasants. People like these belonged to a manor community. ➤

He lived in a virtually impregnable castle, and had what amounted to his own small private army. Nearly everyone who lived on his land owed him some kind of service, and had to obey whatever laws he chose to lay down, on pain of either death or imprisonment.

In return for the powers he had been given over his area of land, the baron had to do homage to his lord, the King. He also had to pay certain taxes and various other dues which were strictly laid down under feudal law. But most important of all, he had to supply a stated number of knights and other well-trained men-at-arms, to assist the King in battle whenever he needed them.

The tenants-in-chief did not look after all their land themselves, however. Each estate was divided up into numerous smaller areas, called manors, and about two thirds of these were handed over to sub-tenants. Under the feudal system the sub-tenants were vassals of the tenants-in-chief just as the tenants-in-chief were vassals of the King. Each baron promised to protect the land and property of his sub-tenants and, in return, every sub-tenant promised absolute loyalty to the baron both in peace and in war. In particular, the sub-tenant always swore that he would help the baron make up the number of knights and men-at-arms which he was under solemn obligation to provide for the King.

By far the largest class of people in Norman times were the peasants. They were divided into three distinct groups — the villeins, the cottars and the serfs. The best-off were the villeins. They held a certain number of strips of land in the manor fields, in which they could grow food for themselves, and in return, they had to work at least three days a week on the lord of the manor's estate. The cottars also had some land, but not enough to grow all

and well-equipped fighting force. Under the feudal system the King owned all the land in the country, and all the rest of the people, however rich and important they might be, were only his tenants and sub-tenants.

The tenants-in-chief were those who held their land directly from the King. In early Norman times these tenants-in-chief were the French and Norman barons who had encouraged William to conquer the country. There were only about one hundred and eighty of them to share the land immediately after the Conquest, which meant that each was responsible for a very considerable area of the country. On his own estate the baron had almost regal powers.

the food they needed, and so they scraped together a living as best they could by hiring themselves out as labourers whenever they had the chance. The serfs had no land at all and as they were legally slaves, they had no choice, either, about what kind of work they should do, or where they should live.

All these three groups of peasants were supposed to be ready to take up arms for the baron, but, in fact, most of the cottars and serfs were too ignorant and slow-witted to be of any use as fighting men. Only the villeins were ever called to the

colours, and even then the barons usually preferred a troop of trained mercenaries to a crowd of villagers who could probably not be relied upon to obey orders.

At first the Saxons naturally hated their Norman conquerors. Indeed, resistance lasted several years before the whole of the country was finally settled and peaceful. But the Saxons soon realized that Norman rule had many good features, especially under such a strong and able king as William the Conqueror. Because the Normans were extremely good lawmakers and strong rulers, ordinary people were able to go about

vi. **TERRA EPI WELLENSIS**

Eps Wellensis ten Welle. Ipse tenuit T.B.E.
7 geldb p. l. hid. Tra e. lx. car. De ea se in dnio. viii.
hide. 7 ibi. vi. car. 7 vi. serui. 7 xx. uilli 7 xxvi. bord.
cu. xx. car. Ibi. iiii. molini redd. xxx. solid. 7 ccc. ac pa.
Pastura. iii. leu lg. 7 una leu lat. Silua. ii. leu lg.
7 ii. ac lat. 7 iii. leu moræ. Valet. xxx. lib. ad op epi.
De hac tra eid as ten canonici. xviii. hid. Ibi hnt
in dnio. vi. car. 7 viii. serui. 7 xxvi. uilli 7 xii. bord.
cu. viii. car. Ibi. ii. molini redd. l. den. Valet. xii. lib.
De ead tra eid as ten de epo Fastrad. vi. hid. Ricard
v. hid. Erneis. v. hid. Ibi st in dnio. vi. car. 7 x. serui.
7 xvii. uilli. 7 xxvi. bord. cu xii. car. 7 iii. molini redd.
x. solid. Int oms ualet. xiii. lib.

4 The Norman rulers brought order to the government of England. They carried out a survey of all the land and inhabitants of England and the information was recorded in the Domesday Book. This is an extract from the Domesday Book on Somerset. It was written in Latin. Notice the strange handwriting.

5 The chest in which the Domesday Book was kept.

their business in safety and trade and commerce could flourish. Taxes were certainly heavier than they had been before the Conquest, but as time went on people could see the result of this in a better-ordered society.

Unlike some conquerors, the Normans did not keep themselves apart from the people they had conquered, either. They tried to teach the Saxons the Norman language, and helped them to adapt themselves to Norman manners and customs. The Normans were also willing to intermarry with the Saxons and, as a result, long before the Norman period had come to an end, the differences between the two races were fast disappearing.

The Normans were devout Christians. They built churches in almost every part of the country, which quickly became the

6 In architecture too the Norman conquerors had a great influence. Here, two of the Norman kings are shown with buildings put up by the Normans: left, William the Conqueror with Battle Abbey; right, William Rufus, his successor, with Westminster Hall.

centres of local community life. When mass had been celebrated, the wooden altar would be carefully moved aside, and all kinds of meetings and other social gatherings would be held in the church. The Normans also built monasteries all over the country. A monastery again formed the centre of community life for the people who lived round about. The monks provided a school for the local boys, nursed the sick and the old and did their best to help anyone who came to them in need or distress.

Above all, the Norman Conquest provided a link between England and the rest

9

of Europe. Indeed, for the first time since the Roman era there was a genuine exchange of ideas between this country and the Continent. England was no longer an unimportant, almost forgotten island, but part of one of the greatest and most powerful realms in the eleventh-century world.

Children in England during the Norman Conquest grew up in a time of great contrasts. For some life must have seemed good; for others it must have appeared bleak and harsh indeed. But it was, in fact, a time when enormous and far-reaching changes were taking place. For a few children, at least, it must have been a time of almost unlimited opportunities.

7 The Norman cathedral at Southwell, Nottinghamshire. Rounded arches are the best-known feature of Norman architecture.

10

2 Growing up in a Castle

The castle buildings

The first castles the Normans built in this country were made of wood. They were thrown up in an enormous hurry to help the Normans subdue any uprisings of the Saxons. In fact, some of the castles had even been prefabricated in France; the pieces were shipped across the Channel and only needed assembling in this country.

The Normans always built their castles on the top of a small hill. This gave them the advantage of being able to shoot downwards on any attackers. If they could not find a natural hill suitable, they would force the unfortunate people whom they had conquered to build an artificial mound, called a motte.

At first a Norman castle consisted simply of a keep on top of a motte. But later on an outer courtyard — called the bailey — was added on one side of the motte. By this time the castles were built of stone and heavily fortified, and usually had a deep moat round them which could be crossed only when the drawbridge was down.

The keep remained the strongest, best-guarded part of the castle, though. It usually had four or five floors (linked by a spiral staircase) and strongly fortified battlements on the top. In the basement were store-rooms and dungeons, above them the guardroom and chapel, above these the great hall, and on the top floor the bedrooms and dormitories. In times of war or siege everyone would crowd together inside the

8 The men inside the castle built on a hill have the advantage over the attackers from below.

9 Building an artificial hill, or motte, for the castle at Hastings.

11

keep. They knew that they could hold out there as long as their provisions and ammunition lasted. But in peace time only the baron's family and a few soldiers lived in the keep. All the other castle servants and retainers lived and worked in wooden huts in the bailey.

A morning in the castle

The day began in a castle at sunrise, if not before. A watchman unfurled a banner on top of the keep, and blew a few loud notes on his horn. This was intended to wake not only the servants but also all the baron's family, for everyone, regardless of rank, got up as soon as it was light, in both winter and summer.

The children put on their undergarments and washed their hands and faces. There was only cold water and no soap, but they liked to keep themselves as clean as they could. When they had dressed, they folded

◄ 10   The keep of Castle Hedingham, Essex.

11   Harlech Castle. The keep is protected by fortified walls round the bailey, and there is a ditch, or moat, around the walls.

up their straw mattresses and their thick woollen blankets (they had no sheets or any other form of bedding) and went to the chapel for mass. At least one of the clerks at the castle was a priest, and mass was normally said every morning — not just on Sundays and feast days. During the service all the important people usually lay face downwards on the floor with their arms outstretched, in the shape of a cross, while the servants and soldiers knelt together at the back of the chapel.

After mass everyone had breakfast. The older children in the baron's family (from about seven years old upwards) then began their lessons with one of the clerks. For most of the boys, however, the most exciting, important part of the day was the afternoon, when they went out with some of the grown-up men to practise hunting and shooting.

14

12 One of the rooms in the keep at Castle Hedingham. The door and the huge fireplace are rounded in Norman style. But you can imagine the cold and discomfort of living in rooms like this.

Hunting

In Norman times hunting had not become a sport. Even for noble people it was still mainly a means of obtaining fresh meat, particularly when it was scarce in the winter. But it must have been fun for the boys (and sometimes the girls) to gallop over the baron's great estates with their bows and arrows, and to see which of them could bring home the biggest bag of game.

Rich boys were also taught hawking or falconry. This was a type of hunting in which falcons were used to catch smaller birds. The boy put a thick gauntlet on his hand on which the falcon perched. He then sent the falcon up into the air, and after hovering for a few moments it would pounce down on its prey.

14 Harold with hunting dogs and a falcon. The Norman embroiderers of the Bayeux Tapestry have not shown Harold wearing a gauntlet.

◄ **13** Stag hunting.

15 Jousting.

15

Tilting and jousting

In addition a baron's son was always taught tilting and jousting. These were both sports designed to teach boys how to fight on horseback when they grew up. When they were small the boys would just watch other knights taking part in a tournament, but by the time they were about twelve or thirteen years old they would usually join in the tournament themselves. In tilting you galloped on horseback towards a quintain. This was an upright post, with a cross-piece at the top which could swing round. On one end of this cross-piece was a board, rather

16 Five different types of musical instrument.

like a shield. At the other end hung a sand-bag. The rider charged at the board with his lance and as he hit it, the cross-piece turned round. If the rider did not gallop on past quickly enough, he was likely to be knocked off his horse by the sand-bag. In jousting the aim was for one knight to try to unseat another from his horse, although there was always a low fence between the two combatants to try to prevent them from inflicting any serious wounds on each other.

16

17 Bagpipes.

Evenings

When evening came all the children would return to the castle. After supper they would usually sit together for an hour or two with the rest of the family in the great hall. They would often sing, or perhaps play some musical instruments. The Normans loved music and the better-off families always encouraged their children to learn to play an instrument if they could. The favourite instruments at that time were the harp, fiddle, flute and cymbals. Among the wind instruments, bagpipes, bassoons, trombones and trumpets were probably the most popular. There were also the regals (a kind of small portable organ), the double pipes, and sets of handbells, which many of the children learnt to play.

No one sat up very late in Norman times. Unless there were guests or it was a feast day, even adults usually went to bed quite soon after it became dark. The reason was that the only means of lighting known at that period were rush-lights and candles. Not only did these make the atmosphere smoky and smelly, but also they gave such a poor light that a large part of every room must still always have been in shadow after dark.

Coming of age for a baron's son

When a baron's son came of age there was always a great feast. But it was only the eldest son, the heir to the barony, who had a secure future. Any younger sons, if they did not want to become monks, usually ended up as mercenaries, fighting for any baron who happened to need some knights to assist him.

◄ **18** Handbells.

3 Growing up in a Manor House

The land held by a Norman baron sometimes amounted to an area as large as a modern county. What was more, his land was usually scattered, in numerous small manors, across the whole country. Clearly, the baron could not look after all this land himself, and so he generally put stewards in charge of a certain number of the manors, and handed over the remainder to sub-tenants, called sokemen or socmen.

Legally, the baron was always the lord of all the manors, of course. But most of the local peasants must have regarded as their lord the steward or sokeman who looked after their particular manor. He lived in the manor house in just as much comfort and ease as the baron did in his castle (and sometimes more), although a steward might occasionally have to move out when the baron came to visit the manor.

The manor house

The average manor house was a solid building of timber and clay. It was surrounded by various smaller outbuildings, such as the kitchen, dairies, store-rooms and stables. There was a large courtyard, enclosed by a stout fence or stockade with only one gate, so that no one could come in without being noticed and, perhaps, stopped and questioned.

In early Norman times the house often consisted of one large hall. In the middle was a hearth in a long trench, and a hole in the roof to let out the smoke. At one end of the hall was a dais, which was the dining area for the family and the more important

guests. The servants and everyone else would eat in the lower part of the hall.

Along all four sides of the hall there were wooden pillars supporting the roof, and in between these a number of small alcoves or bays were formed. During the day these alcoves provided extra living space for the family, but at night curtains were drawn across them, so that each of them became a small, private bedroom. The steward, or sokeman, and his wife slept in the alcove behind the dais. Their sons slept in another alcove nearby and their daughters and any babies or toddlers in another. There were nearly always people sleeping in the other alcoves as well, for, as there were no inns where anyone could stay in Norman times, travellers constantly asked for a night's lodging at a manor house.

It must have been interesting for the children of the manor house to meet so many different visitors. For example, there would sometimes be a Norman knight, who could never be turned away, because the Normans were so important and powerful. There might be a merchant, who would probably have several servants with him, as well as a train of pack ponies, which would have to be unloaded and tied up for the night in the courtyard. Occasionally a priest might come, although priests needing lodgings would probably prefer to spend the night in a monastery. In addition, pilgrims

19 The Hall of a Norman manor house, showing the hearth in the centre of the floor, and the dais where the family would eat.

on their way to visit a shrine or some other holy place would quite often ask to stay the night at the manor house. And almost every day there came pedlars, with packs on their backs — although the stewards and sokemen were not always anxious to take in people of this kind, in case they turned out to be thieves.

20 Travelling pedlars — less welcome visitors to the manor.

21 A reeve supervises the reapers, with their curved sickles, who are working on the lord of the manor's estate.

Lessons

The children in a manor house usually had their lessons at home. They were taught by a clerk, and had much the same kind of education as the children in a castle. It was important, at least for the boys, to be able to read and write Latin, for otherwise they would not be able to manage the complicated affairs of the manor when they grew up. In the afternoon the boys did not go hunting like the sons of a baron, though. Instead, they usually spent most of their time helping their fathers on the manor. Although there was no law that a sokeman's son should inherit the manor when his father died, most boys naturally hoped that they would do so, and even a steward's son generally expected to take over his father's position.

The reeve

The main task of the steward or sokeman was to see that the manor was farmed efficiently. For this he relied heavily on the assistance of a man called a reeve. Generally, every year or two, the villeins of the manor chose one man from among themselves to be reeve. It was his job to share out the work which had to be done on the manor among all the various peasants. To a large extent the happiness and contentment of the peasants depended on the reeve. At ploughing time, for instance, he would decide how much seed the villeins had to provide for the manor, and when they would have to bring their ploughs and their oxen. But the average reeve probably did his best to be fair, because he knew that one of the other villeins would be the reeve, telling him what to do himself, in a year or two's time!

The miller and the blacksmith

The children of the steward or sokeman did not often play with the peasants' children, but there were various other children who lived on the manor and who were regarded as more or less their social equals. These were the children of such people as the miller, the blacksmith and the shepherd, who were all men of some substance in Norman times, and probably much envied by the ordinary villeins.

21

▲
22   A corn handmill.

The miller, for instance, had the right to grind all the corn on the manor. This often annoyed the villeins, who would rather have ground their corn themselves on a small handmill. They were forced to take the corn to the miller, who kept some of it for himself as his fee, and also passed some on to the lord of the manor as rent. The blacksmith, on the other hand, was often considered a kind of witch-doctor. Everyone knew that he had charms which could cure headaches and toothaches and perhaps even stop bleeding as well. The average villein had little hope of ever becoming a miller or blacksmith himself, of course, because these jobs (just like the posts of steward and

◄ **23   Blacksmith (see also picture 3).**

24 The woman has toothache and is asking a doctor for help. But on the manor, the blacksmith might be asked for a cure for such a pain.

sokeman) were normally always passed on from father to son.

The manor court

One of the chief tasks of a steward or sokeman was to maintain law and order in his manor. For this he held a manor court, either in the manor house or in the open air, several times every year. The court dealt with minor civil matters, such as disputes over property between two villeins, and with small criminal cases, such as the theft of a hen or a few eggs by a cottar or serf. More serious matters were sent to the hundred court (a hundred was a sub-division of a shire). Or they might even be sent to the shire court, presided over by the shire reeve (or sheriff) and the bishop. But it was to the manor court that the average peasant looked for justice, and if the steward or sokeman made fair, honest decisions, he and his family were naturally held in the greatest esteem by all the local peasantry.

4 Growing up in the Country

The villeins and their land

About forty villeins and their families lived on the average manor. They each held about twelve hectares of land which they were allowed to cultivate for themselves. The land each villein held was not all in one large piece, however, but was divided into a number of long, narrow strips, in at least three separate fields.

The land was divided into fields so that crops could be rotated. The Normans knew nothing about fertilizers, and so it was essential to rotate the crops if they were to continue to give a good yield and the soil was to stay healthy. In any one year, for example, one field would be growing root crops such as turnips or carrots, another would be producing corn or beans, and a third would be lying fallow (resting). The following year the same crops would be grown in different fields. Because he had one or more strips of land in each field, a villein was able to grow a variety of produce each year. Also, the system of strips meant that all the villeins had an equal share of whatever fertile soil there might be and of the poorer soil.

A villein could spend only three days of the week working on his own strips of land, however. On the other three working days he had to work for the lord of the manor, unless it had been agreed that he could pay a certain sum of money instead. He was never allowed to work on a Sunday, either for the lord or for himself, as the Church strictly forbade anyone to do any manual work on the Sabbath.

Jobs for the villein's children

A villein was naturally very glad when his children were old enough to help him. One of the first jobs the children did (from the age of about five or six) was to go into the fields to scare the birds away from the growing corn. They would beat large wooden clappers and shout, and sometimes some of the older children would even try to kill some of the birds by slinging pebbles at them out of their catapults.

Children were also sent into the woods to collect firewood. In the autumn they often

25   Models in the Science Museum, London, of peasants working on the land attached to the manor. In the background you can see the manor house, the church and the villeins' cottages with their thatched roofs.

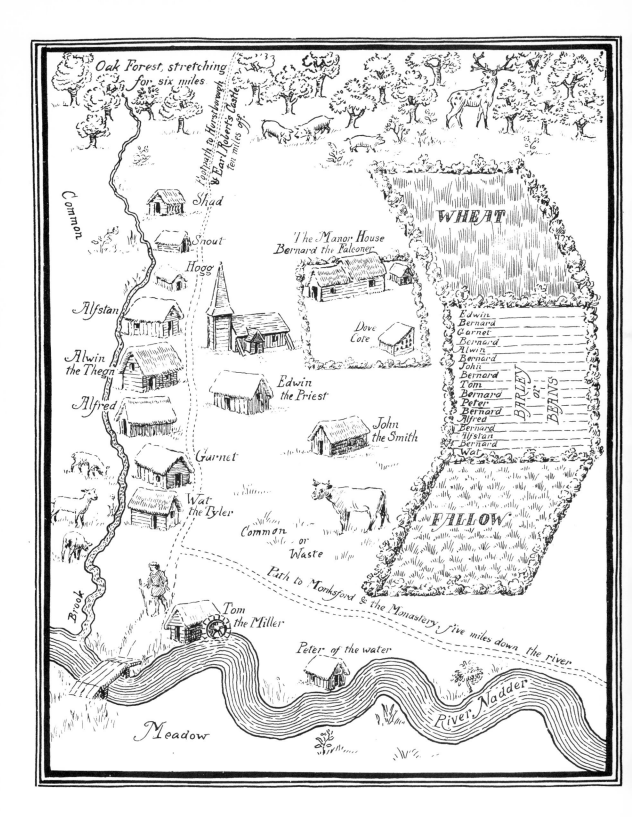

Oak Forest, stretching for six miles

Footpath to Hurstbourne & Earl Roberts Castle, ten miles off

Common

Shad

Snout

Hogg

Alfstan

Alwin the Thegn

Alfred

Garnet

Wat the Tyler

The Manor House Bernard the Falconer

WHEAT

Dove Cote

Edwin the Priest

John the Smith

Edwin
Bernard
Garnet
Bernard
Alwin
Bernard
John
Bernard
Tom
Bernard
Peter
Bernard
Alfred
Bernard
Alfstan
Bernard
Wat

BARLEY or BEANS

FALLOW

Common or Waste

Brook

Path to Monksford & the Monastery, five miles down the river

Tom the Miller

Peter of the water

River Nadder

Meadow

◄ 26   The strip system. You can see how a number of strips of the big field were allotted to the inhabitants of the manor.

27   This sower has only his dog to scare away the birds. The children often helped to keep the birds away from the corn.

collected acorns and beech-nuts as well, as food for the pigs. At ploughing time it was the children's job to hold the goads to urge on the oxen, and at harvest time some of the boys took it in turn to turn the grindstone for the men to sharpen their sickles.

Another important job done by the boys was to keep their fathers' arrow-heads clean. This meant rubbing them with sand every two or three weeks so that they were always bright and sharp. The villein needed his bow and arrows in case he was ever called upon by the baron to take up arms. But many barons preferred to employ trained mercenaries rather than ask for help from only semi-trained peasants.

When a boy was about sixteen years old he was regarded as being a man. This meant that he could take a turn helping on the lord of the manor's estate so that his father would have more time to work on his own land. Shortly after this the boy might marry (peasants usually married while they were still very young), although he would have to get the permission of the lord of the manor first, especially if he wanted to marry a girl from a different manor.

28   Armed with bow and arrow.

The villein's cottage

A villein usually lived in a one-roomed cottage. Its walls were made of wattle and daub, and its thatched roof formed wide eaves that overhung the walls on all sides. There were no windows, but light came in through the doorway, which could be closed at night with a leather curtain (there was no proper door).

Inside the cottage the floor was made of hard earth. In the centre there was a flat hearthstone, and a fire of wood or turf was kept burning most of the time. There was a hole in the roof above the fire which let out some of the smoke, but even so the cottage was usually very smelly and smoky, particularly in the winter.

The furniture in a cottage was very roughly fashioned. A board on trestles formed the table, and a few chests (in which the family kept all their possessions) served as seats. In one corner there was a pile of straw on which the whole family slept, side by side, covered with some old clothes or perhaps a few skins.

The cottages were usually filthy. There were always great dung-heaps beside the door, and hens and even pigs were allowed to live with the family. In the summer

29 A woman warming herself by the fire. This carving is on a folding seat, or misericord, in Ludlow Parish Church.

conditions were generally a little better, though, as people usually spent most of their time in the open, and even slept out-of-doors under the eaves of their cottages.

A villein's family did not often go short of food. But if the harvest was poor, they might only have enough grain to make bread, and have none left over to make ale. This meant that everyone in the family had to drink water instead, and as the water was often contaminated with sewage or rubbish a certain number of people (particularly children) were poisoned by it and died.

The cottars and serfs

Another group of poor country people were the cottars. They lived in even worse hovels than the villeins, and had only a small piece of land on which to grow a few vegetables. The cottars relied for their living almost entirely on being hired by the lord of the manor as herdsmen or labourers, and when work was short they were often in danger of starving.

The third group of country people were the serfs, or slaves. These were the people who had no land at all, but just lived and worked on their master's estate. According to the law, a serf had no rights of any kind and could at any time be sold by his master, against his will, to the lord of some other manor. In practice, however, the serfs were in some ways better off than the cottars. At least they knew they would always have enough food to eat and somewhere to sleep. Also, the Church insisted that even the serfs should have certain basic rights as Christians, such as being allowed to marry and bring up a family, and it tried to ensure that the serfs were properly treated.

The children of the villeins, cottars and serfs had one thing in common. It was most unlikely that during the whole of their childhood they would ever go more than a kilometre or two outside their own village. The only reason they would ever go further afield would be to be confirmed by the bishop in the nearest big town, but this only happened if they had a very enterprising parish priest.

30 The beggar at the feast. Really poor people had to beg for food at the gates of castles and richer houses.

5 Growing up in a Town

London

Easily the biggest town in Norman England was London. Its population was well over ten thousand, probably more than twice that of any other town in England in those days. One of William's first acts after he had conquered the country was to begin building a great castle, now the famous Tower of London, to help defend his new capital.

31 Norman builders at work. Here they are working on St Albans Abbey.

32   A monk in a shop.

The townspeople

There were, however, a number of other sizeable towns in England. Like London, they nearly all depended for a great deal of their prosperity on commerce and trade. As a result many of the richest townspeople were merchants, dealing in anything from salted fish from Norway to jewellery from Constantinople. As well as the merchants, a large number of prosperous craftsmen lived in the town with their journeymen (or assistants) and their apprentices, and there were a great many unskilled artisans of various kinds. Some of these unskilled artisans were serfs, who had escaped from a manor, and hoped to be able to stay in the town for at least a year and a day, for at the end of that time they would be legally free.

All the well-to-do townspeople were officially the King's tenants. But instead of supplying him with fighting men (as in the case of the barons — page 6), they paid him a fixed sum of money every year. Nevertheless, most townspeople would willingly have helped to defend their town, and most of them had at least a large, two-handed axe at home, if not a full set of chainmail and a sword.

Houses

A well-to-do merchant or craftsman lived in a two-storeyed, wooden house. Its frontage was often about 12-20 metres, and the house usually extended quite a long way to the rear. On the ground floor, on the street side, there was a shop or workshop, and above that a solar (the principal living-room of the house). At the back were a large hall and all the rest of the living quarters.

Round three sides of the house there was a large piece of ground. Part of this was used as a courtyard, and the rest was

32

generally dug up and used as a kitchen garden. Although townspeople bought most of their food (including their bread) from the shops and markets, they nearly always liked to have their own home-grown vegetables if it was possible.

The outbuildings around the house included a shed, with a large hearth in the middle, which was the family's kitchen. This was always built as far away from the house as possible so that if there were a fire in the kitchen it would not spread to the main house. One of the greatest dangers in a town where all the buildings were made of timber was an accidental fire.

The adults in the family usually slept on straw mattresses in the loft. But the children generally just curled up on some straw in a corner of the solar. There was a curfew in most of the towns, so it was always very quiet at night, except for the cries of the watchman calling out the time and the weather.

Apprentices

As soon as he was old enough, a craftsman's son generally wanted to work with his father. In most cases he began by serving some of the customers, so that his father could get on with making more goods to sell. Some boys wanted to follow quite a different trade from the rest of their family, though, and then they usually became apprentices, probably when they were about eleven or twelve years old.

In Norman times there was no definite period laid down that a boy had to spend as an apprentice. He simply found a craftsman who would accept him, and worked for him until he thought he had mastered the trade. There were no strictly laid down agreements between a master and an appren-

33 This house in Lincoln was originally a Norman merchant's house. You can see the Norman-style rounded arches. But it has been much altered since.

tice, either. The boy probably received some pocket money, and the craftsman would also have provided him with free board and lodging. When the boy's training was finished his master took him before a group of fellow craftsmen. He vouched for the boy's ability, and the boy was duly recognized as a master craftsman himself. There were no craft guilds in early Norman times, as there were later, so, in fact, nothing could stop anyone from setting himself up as a craftsman without serving any apprenticeship at all, if he wished.

▲
34   Carpenters.

▲
35   People coming to the market from surrounding villages might have transported their goods in carts like this.

Like everyone else, an apprentice had to work from dawn till dusk. The working day during the summer months must have seemed very long indeed. There was nothing for a boy to do after work, though, unless he wanted to meet some of his friends in a tavern, as there was no entertainment of any kind in the evenings. There were fortunately several holy days every month when no one did any work. But apart from these there were no regular holidays, not even during the summer. The longest break of the year for the apprentices (and for everyone else in the towns) was the Christmas holiday, which lasted from Christmas Day till Twelfth Night.

36 It looks as if the woman is trying to barter a cup for some clothes.

Markets and fairs

There was always plenty of excitement in the towns for the children, though. Every Sunday, for instance, a market was held. (Sunday was the most popular day for a market all through the Norman period.) It was usually held in the square in front of the parish church, and small-holders and their wives from all the surrounding villages brought their produce to be sold.

Even more exciting than the markets was the annual fair. This always lasted for several days, and took place on a piece of waste ground a little way outside the town. At a fair you found not only local people selling their wares, but traders from all over the country too, and sometimes even from abroad, with all kinds of rare and exotic goods.

Nothing on sale at a market or fair ever had a price on it. The buyer and seller haggled between themselves until they agreed on a sum that seemed reasonable. Very often money was not used at all. Instead, people fell back on the centuries-old custom of bartering, just exchanging one article for another.

Very few children were ever given any money to spend. The smallest coin in Norman times was a silver penny, and that was all the average working man earned in a day. People sometimes cut the coins into four (they had a cross on the back to make cutting easier), but even a quarter of a penny was quite a large amount to most families at that period.

37 A silver penny, with the head of William the ► Conqueror.

6 Education

Not everyone in England in Norman times spoke the same language. The Norman barons, for example, usually spoke only French, and knew perhaps a smattering of English. The rest of the better-off people spoke either French or English, according to whether they were of Norman or Saxon descent, while the Saxon peasants naturally spoke English only.

To complicate matters even more, all the books were written in Latin. But very few people, except monks, ever managed to read Latin really fluently. Therefore, only a small number of people, even among those who were considered educated, could pick up any book they wished and read it easily, for either pleasure or information.

Education of the well-to-do

A baron's son began his education at the age of seven. His tutor was generally one of the clerks employed to keep the castle's records and accounts. Sometimes a boy was given his lessons alone, but more often than not three or four children in a baron's family were all able to do their schoolwork together.

The children had lessons in the mornings only. (In the afternoons they learnt to ride or to shoot, or practised some other knightly pursuit.) They did not have a special schoolroom, but usually worked in a small hut in the bailey, where the clerks also had to do all their work connected with the castle.

The children usually wrote on smooth tablets of beechwood. Their pens were sharpened quills, and the ink was a mixture of water and soot. The clerks, on the

38   A doctor instructs his pupil on making a ➤ drug.

other hand, wrote on parchment, but this was so expensive that whenever possible it was sponged clean after use, and written on again and again.

The children first had to learn Latin. They were accustomed to hearing it spoken, by both the clerks and the priests in the chapel, but they usually had little idea of the grammar, and even less of the way in which the words ought to be spelt and written down. One of the chief difficulties in learning to read Latin was that there were so many contractions and abbreviations. In fact, reading Latin was often like trying to understand some odd kind of shorthand. Moreover, all the books were written by hand by the monks, and the handwriting of the monks in one monastery might be completely different from the handwriting of the monks in another.

If the boys did not work hard at their lessons, they were beaten. Every teacher kept a stout stick and used it to thrash the boys across the shoulders when they deserved it. It was a point of honour among well-born boys not to cry out and so allow the lowly born clerk to think that they were unable to accept pain bravely.

By the age of twelve a rich boy was thought to have completed his education. By then he could usually understand the various legal documents to which he might later have to put his seal, and this was considered sufficient. There was also a

growing feeling among noble families that it was slightly beneath their dignity to spend too much time on books, and that learning should be left to the monks and the clerks.

Schools in the towns

Boys who lived in a town also began their education at the age of about seven. Mostly they went to a school maintained by a monastery, or perhaps by a very large church. The master of the school (there was usually only one master) was sometimes a monk or a priest, but quite often just a secular clerk.

The standard of education in these schools naturally varied greatly. In some of them the boys learnt virtually nothing, except a little elementary reading and writing. In others the masters were well-known scholars, and the standard was so high that boys were sent to these schools from every part of the country.

When the teaching was more advanced, the curriculum was based on the education in Ancient Rome. (All the teaching was, of course, conducted entirely in Latin.) First the students studied the Trivium, which was grammar, rhetoric and logic, and then the

37

S. ANSELMVS ARCHIEPISCOPVS CANTVARIENSIS.
Monachus Benedictinus. April. 21.   M. haes.

Quadrivium, which was music, arithmetic, geometry and astronomy.

The most famous school of all was undoubtedly the one at Oxford. Towards the end of the Norman period it is said to have had nearly three thousand pupils, and must have had a large number of masters. There were also several well-known schools in London, and on feast days the boys from the various schools often had competitions against each other in grammar and rhetoric.

University

Outstandingly gifted boys sometimes went on to the university. In Norman times this always meant going abroad, as there were no recognized centres of higher education in our country at that time. Boys who wanted to study law nearly always went to Bologna University, in Italy, while boys who wished to study other subjects went to Paris, or later to Chartres (also in France). Boys who wanted to study theology, however, usually went to Le Bec, in Normandy. This was a highly regarded seat of learning attached to a famous monastery. Two of the masters there, Lanfranc and Anselm, who were both of Italian origin, both in turn rose to become Archbishop of Canterbury.

As all the students spoke Latin, students from all over Europe could easily study together. The rich rented rooms near the university, or even houses, and brought their own servants to wait on them. The poor, however, had to find jobs in order to pay their fees and to keep themselves. They often took posts giving tuition to the sons of rich noblemen.

Education for the peasants

Even the sons of peasants had the chance of going to school in Norman times. In nearly every village the local parish priest gave reading and writing lessons in the parish church. Any reasonably intelligent boys (or even sometimes girls) could attend, providing that they began at the age of seven or eight, for it was thought to be almost impossible to teach a person over that age to become literate.

39 Anselm, Archbishop of Canterbury.

7 The Children of the Cloister

In Saxon times a boy had entered a monastery when he was only seven years old, and he had immediately taken permanent vows, binding himself to remain a monk for the rest of his life. If later on he changed his mind and tried to leave the monastery, he was not only excommunicated by the Church but he also became an outlaw in the eyes of the civil authority.

After the Norman Conquest boys still entered the monasteries at the age of seven, but they were not allowed to make any permanent, binding vows until they were at least sixteen years old. Up to that age they could leave the monastery whenever they wished, although they might have to repay the money which the monks had spent on looking after them and on educating them during the time they had been there.

40 Remains of Rievaulx Abbey.

◄ **41 A young boy is tonsured.**

These boy monks were known as the children of the cloister. They nearly all came from prosperous, upper-class families, and were often the children of barons. This was not because the monasteries would not accept poor boys, but because most poor parents needed all their children to stay and help them on the land and to support them in their old age. Rich parents, on the other hand, wanted all their wealth to pass on to their eldest son only, because that way their estates would not be broken up and would remain large and important. They were therefore only too pleased for their younger sons to go into monasteries, where they knew they would be well looked after and well educated, among other young men from the same station in life.

42 Monks who misbehaved were put in stocks. Notice the handwriting of this manuscript.

As soon as a boy entered a monastery his hair was closely cropped and at the same time he was given a tonsure (a small, round shaved patch on the crown of the head). The boy had to wear the long, black robes of a monk, although his habit did not have a cowl (hood) attached to it until he had taken his final vows. Round his waist he wore a girdle of either rope or leather. To this he could attach a small purse or wallet, in which he could keep any little odds and ends. As the boys were not vowed to poverty like the adult monks, their parents sometimes sent them a little pocket money, or perhaps a few sweets or toys.

There might be forty or more boys in a large monastery. They all slept, ate and worked together, and were never normally allowed to speak to the adult monks. The only monk they usually knew was the novice-master. He took complete charge of them, and if they disobeyed him in even the slightest way he would flog them. The boys were not expected to behave like grown-up monks, though. They were expected only to act like any other well-behaved, well-brought-up boys of their age. They were given various privileges, such as being allowed to go for rambles on Sundays and other feast days, while the adult monks usually had to stay strictly within the monastery grounds.

A day in the monastery

The day for the adult monks began at two o'clock in the morning, but the boys were allowed to stay in bed at least one hour and sometimes two hours longer than

this. Then they had to join the adult monks in the chapel for the first office (or service) of the day, which usually went on until about six o'clock. The boys then went to the refectory for a breakfast of bread and milk. The adult monks, however, were never allowed to eat anything before their main meal at midday. At 8.00 a.m. the High Mass was celebrated — the most important service of the day, which nearly all the boys had to attend because they were needed to sing in the choir.

Afterwards the boys went to the cloisters to begin their lessons. By the time they arrived some of the senior boys would have already put up several long trestle tables. Although there were plenty of servants in the monastery (all men or boys, of course, so that they could live within the enclosure), it was considered good training for the older boys to have to do small jobs like this.

When the boys first arrived at the monastery they were allowed to speak French or English. But within a year or two at the most they were strictly forbidden to speak any language other than Latin. So, the boys' most important task when they first entered the monastery was to learn to think and speak in Latin just as clearly and fluently as they did in their mother tongue. The boys then had to learn to read and write. Writing was particularly important, as many of them would have to spend countless hours in the

43 Monks in cloisters. The cloisters were arched passageways round a square yard. The monks used to work in the cloisters where there was light and fresh air and shelter.

44 A monk writing.

as the wine which the monks drank was considered to be too strong and too expensive to be given to children.

After dinner everyone had a rest for an hour or two. Then, at about half past two, there were some more prayers in the chapel, and at three o'clock the boys had to go on with their lessons again. At about 5.30 p.m. the boys had supper, and at about 8.00 p.m. everyone, both boys and adult monks, went to bed for the night.

When the boys finally took their vows most of them became choir monks. This meant that they spent the majority of their time in the chapel, taking part in all the various services. In later Norman times, however, there were all kinds of other tasks the monks could undertake, from being in charge of the monastery's wine cellar to being in charge of the whole of the monastery's estates.

future copying out books by hand for the monastery library. The boys also learnt to sing and to read music, so that they could take part in all the monastery's services, and some of them also learnt to play a musical instrument.

At midday everyone stopped work and went to dinner. The boys ate in their own refectory seated on either side of a long table, with the novice-master at the head. Like the adult monks, the boys were not allowed to talk during the meal, but had to listen to one of the monks reading passages from the Bible or from another holy book. The adult monks were never allowed to eat meat (although they ate poultry and fish), but the boys were quite often given roast mutton, boiled bacon or some similar dish. The boys drank only water or beer, however,

45 Choir of monks.

8 Girls

By modern standards, women and girls led narrow, dull lives in Norman times. They were poorly educated, and were rarely allowed to join in any activities outside the home with their menfolk. Nevertheless they were always treated with respect and courtesy, as the Church was constantly emphasizing the importance of their role as wives and mothers.

46 Mother and child, from a 12th-century bible. The Church stressed that women should be respected.

Well-born girls

A baron's daughter often shared her first lessons with her brothers. She would learn to read and write (in Latin), and might even learn to ride and to hunt. When she was a little older she might be sent to a local convent, where the nuns would teach her to sew and embroider, and usually also to sing and play a musical instrument.

In a castle the women and girls had a special bower. This was a small timber building in the bailey, which the men and boys were never allowed to enter. The baron's wife and her daughters spent a large part of the day there, engaged in sewing or embroidery, while one of their more educated women attendants read aloud to them from a good book.

When a well-born girl was eleven or twelve years old she was betrothed, and then probably quite soon after her thirteenth birthday she was considered old enough to

47 A nun confessing her sins to a monk.

get married. Her husband had to be someone of equal social rank with her, but whether she liked him, let alone loved him, was not considered important.

The only alternative to marriage was to become a nun. However, most of the convents in early Norman times were rather small and impoverished. Apart from producing beautiful embroidery (probably the finest in Europe), the nuns had little or no outlet for any other talents or skills they might possess.

Town girls

A girl born in a town usually had much more freedom than a baron's daughter. From the time she was quite small, for example, she would go to the shops or the market with her mother. When she was a little older, she might even go shopping by herself, taking a small stick with her on which the shop-keeper made a notch for each of the purchases, so that her mother could pay for them later. She might also help her mother by keeping an eye on the servants while they were cleaning the house. (Well-to-do townspeople were very anxious not to have dirty, foul-smelling homes like the peasants.) She would make sure, for instance, that the servants had put fresh rushes down on the floor, and that they had scraped away any grease that might have dropped from the rush-lights or candles.

When a girl brought up in a town was about twelve years old it was time for her to get married. Unlike the baron's daughter,

she would be allowed to marry anyone she liked, within reason. She probably did not know her husband very well before they married, though, as young people had very little opportunity to meet and talk, except at church, or perhaps at the home of a friend. A wedding was always a religious ceremony in Norman times, but it did not necessarily have to be performed in church, in front of the altar. What mattered was that a priest should be present and that it should be performed in public. In fact, the porch of the church was a very popular place for weddings in Norman days.

If a girl was still unmarried at sixteen she was considered an old maid. She might decide to enter a convent and become a nun, just like the daughter of a baron. However,

48   A young couple are married.

a girl in a town could sometimes get a job as a seamstress or an embroiderer, if she did not want to marry and felt no call to the religious life.

Country girls

A girl born in the country was certainly never idle or bored. She had jobs to do in and around the house almost from the time she could toddle. Like her brothers she probably began by scaring the birds off the crops, but it would not have been long before she was also feeding the hens and collecting the eggs. Most country girls, while they were still quite small, also learnt to milk a cow. They were not usually strong enough to turn a butter churn, but they would often learn to make cheese. Another task that always fell to the girls was looking after the bees. Honey was extremely important, as it was virtually the only form of sweetening that was known at that period.

49 These men are flailing the corn. Afterwards, the girls would winnow it to separate the grain from the chaff.

A country girl naturally helped her mother in the kitchen. She would be shown how to brew ale, as that was always considered a woman's job in Norman times. In addition, she would peel the rushes and soak them in fat to make the rush-lights. Most country people used rush-lights instead of candles because they were cheaper.

At harvest time, of course, everyone had to lend a hand. Most of the girls probably went to the threshing floor, to watch the men beating the corn with their huge flails. As soon as the men had finished, the girls would use their winnowing fans to make a breeze, which would blow away all the chaff, while only the grain fell to the ground.

With all this work to do a country girl had little time for amusement. But in any case most country girls could not read, and they could not afford the materials to do much sewing or embroidery. They nearly always liked to sing and dance, though, and whenever they met together they would sing their favourite songs and make up simple dancing steps to go with them.

Like all the other girls at this period, a country girl married when she was about twelve years old. She would probably know all the boys who lived round about and would marry for love. Her husband would probably be only sixteen or seventeen years old himself, as a country boy was earning as much money at that age (and was just as capable of supporting a wife) as he would be at any other time in his life.

After marriage a country girl usually continued to live in the same village. She probably had a dozen or more children, but only two or three were likely to survive infancy. Even among well-to-do families infant mortality was extremely high, and for poor families, who were nearly always living in filth and squalor, the chances of all their children reaching manhood was very slim indeed.

50   Dancing to the fiddle.

9 Food and Drink

Food in Norman times was plentiful, but the quality, by modern standards, even in a rich baron's home, was often poor. Also, the food eaten lacked variety, as there was no satisfactory method of preserving food so that it could be eaten out of season, and there was no way of quickly transporting perishable foods grown in one particular area of the country to different parts of England.

Breakfast

Breakfast was always a light meal. No one thought of sitting down to it, or of spending more than a few minutes eating it. Even a wealthy family would only have a few slices of a fine white bread, made from wheat, with a little wine, or perhaps some beer or mead for the men and boys. Country people occasionally ate a bowl of porridge for breakfast. But most ordinary working people just had a few crusts of rye bread and some ale. The children ate much the same food as the adults, except that they were sometimes given milk to drink instead of beer, if their family were lucky enough to own a cow or a goat.

51   Servants prepare the food and carry it from the separate kitchens to the dining hall.

52 An oven.

53 Slaughtering a cow.

Midday meal

The main meal of the day was normally taken at midday. Among wealthy people it was usually a very substantial meal indeed.

It was cooked in the castle kitchens, which were in a separate small wooden building in the bailey, and carried into the great hall of the keep by the servants.

During the spring and summer all the rich families had plenty of fresh meat. They usually preferred roast beef, but they also ate some mutton and pork. For a change, they sometimes had partridge or other small birds, if the fowlers had managed to catch any, or occasionally a chicken, a goose or a duck. When autumn came practically all the farm animals had to be slaughtered as the Normans found it impossible to provide enough foodstuff for all their beasts during the cold weather. This meant that even the wealthiest people had to eat salted meat during the winter, but they tried to disguise its unpleasant taste by smothering it in spices, which were imported from the East.

Numerous meatless days were laid down by the Church. These included every Friday, every weekday during Advent and Lent, and the vigils of all the great feast days. Castles and monasteries often had their own fish-ponds, which they always kept well stocked with fish to eat on the meatless days.

Even the less well-off spent considerable time over their midday meal. All the members of the family would sit round a low table together, with a big iron cooking-pot in the centre. The father would say grace, and the whole family would begin dipping in their long wooden spoons to help themselves to the food straight out of the pot. Beef was too expensive for ordinary people, but there was often mutton or bacon. People eked out the meat by cooking it with beans or some kind of porridge. They also quite often ate cabbage and other green-stuff (usually boiled), which better-off families would have thought fit for the animals only.

During the summer months most country people just took bread and cheese to eat in the fields at midday. But when they could come home to their midday meal they usually had some porridge, some green vegetables and perhaps some berries or fruit.

Occasionally they were lucky enough to catch a rabbit or a pigeon, and then the whole family was able to sit down to a stew, although it was generally rather tasteless and watery.

Evening meal
The evening meal, like breakfast, was normally light. Even a baron's family would probably have only a bowl of soup and some bread. However, there was always plenty of beer, or ale (mulled in the winter), or even some flagons of wine if the family were sufficiently wealthy.

Feasts
From time to time, of course, a baron would give a great feast in the evening. He would sit with his chief guests at a table on the low dais at one end of his great hall. All the other people who lived in the castle, and the less important guests, would sit at long

54 Cooking broth or stew in pots over an open fire.

55 A feast in the 11th century. There is fish on the table. The servants are kneeling and the guests help themselves to food from the spits which the servants have brought in.

trestle tables arranged down the hall at right angles to the high table on the dais. On the high table there was set a cloth and elaborate drinking horns, but there was no cutlery. Everyone brought his own knife and spoon. (Forks were unknown in Norman times.) There were also no plates. People used flat, pancake-shaped loaves of bread as platters, or thick slices from a large loaf, and they either ate them at the end of the meal or threw them to the beggars waiting outside the castle walls (see picture 30).

A feast would often begin with herrings or eels. Then there might be several different types of meat, but never venison as all the deer in England belonged to the King. No green vegetables were ever served in wealthy households, but there would be several different kinds of bread to eat with the meat, and to mop up the gravy. After this the guests might be offered some cheese. This was usually made from skimmed cow's milk or ewe's milk, and was something like a modern cream cheese. Finally nuts, apples and honey would be handed round the high table, but would only be passed to the people sitting at the other tables in the hall if there happened to be any to spare.

The wine at the high table was always

imported from France. It was served out of leather bottles, which often gave it a rather peculiar taste. The rest of the company drank beer, unless there was some wine that had turned slightly sour, as it did very quickly because the leather bottles were not completely airtight.

56 Eel traps.

Easter eggs

Oddly enough, the first Easter eggs date from Norman times. Eggs were not allowed to be eaten during Lent, so the farmers' wives used to collect them and put them on one side. On Good Friday the eggs were boiled in coloured water to dye them, and after they had been blessed by the priest they were eaten on Easter Sunday as part of the great Easter festivities.

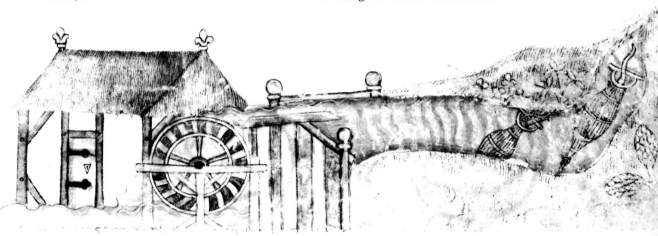

10 Clothes

People had little choice in the style of their clothes in Norman times. Everyone had to dress strictly in accordance with his station in life. The son of a craftsman, for example, would have felt just as embarrassed to be seen dressed like the son of a baron as he would have done to be seen dressed like the son of a serf. There was little choice also in the matter of colour. In early Norman times everyone, rich and poor, dressed almost entirely in drab blues, greens, greys and browns. This was partly because bright dyes were expensive and sometimes crude, but also because bright colours were not the fashion. Bright colours became fashionable towards the end of the Norman period.

Wealthy boys' clothing

A wealthy boy's only undergarment was a pair of long linen drawers. These were shaped rather like modern jodhpurs, loose to the thigh and tight from the knee to the ankle. A strap under the instep kept the drawers from working up as the boy walked,

57 This picture of robbery with violence shows some of the clothing described in this chapter. The men on the left are, of course, in chainmail.

58 In this biblical picture the lady is dressed in 11th-century fashion. You can see the tight sleeves of her kirtle under the wide sleeves of her second tunic. ➤

and a string round the waist took the place of elastic and prevented the drawers from slipping down. The next garment the boy put on was a white woollen shirt. Over this he put on a long-sleeved tunic (often blue) that reached as far as the knees. Round the tunic he wore a narrow leather girdle, but this could not be seen because the upper part of the tunic was always pulled down over it, to make a kind of pocket or pouch.

On his legs a wealthy boy always wore fine woollen puttees. These were strips of cloth wound round and round his calves and knees to make a very elegant criss-cross design. The boy also wore elegant, close-fitting shoes, made of soft leather, with a strap over the instep that was held in place by a metal buckle.

When he went out, a wealthy boy put on an extra tunic or mantle. This usually had wide, three-quarter-length sleeves, and was short enough for the first tunic to show a little way below it. In early Norman times well-to-do boys hardly ever wore any kind of head-dress, except on a long journey in winter, when they might put on a woollen cap or hood.

59 A girl has her hair done in plaits wound round her head.

60 A chin-cloth.

Wealthy girls' clothing

A girl in a wealthy family first put on a plain linen petticoat, and over this a tunic or kirtle, with tight sleeves that reached to the wrist. On top of this the girl wore a second tunic of much the same shape, except that its wide, loose sleeves fell back at the elbow to show the tight sleeves of the kirtle. On her legs she wore woollen stockings of a dull colour such as grey or fawn. These reached well above the knee, and were kept up with woollen garters. The stockings were always woven, as knitting had not been invented in Norman times, and for this reason they were often rather wrinkled and loose round the ankles.

Younger girls nearly always wore their hair in two long plaits. When they were older they usually wound the plaits round their heads, just as their mothers did. They then covered their heads with a white woollen kerchief, which was crossed under their chins to make a frame for the face.

Poorer boys

The son of a merchant or craftsman first put on long drawers as did the rich boy. But over these he put on a thick woollen shirt and a tunic made of coarse, unbleached wool. On his legs he wore knee-length woollen socks, and then woollen puttees, but these were not wound into an elegant pattern as in the case of the wealthy boy.

The son of a villein or serf also wore drawers, but they were woollen, not linen. Over the drawers he wore a low-necked woollen shirt that reached nearly down to his knees. His girdle was not leather, like the rich boy's, but only rope, and he usually had a cowskin wallet attached to it, in which he could keep his odds and ends. On his legs a poor boy wore very coarse woollen puttees, but he usually went barefoot unless the weather was exceptionally cold. Then he sometimes managed to find an old pair of leather shoes; otherwise he would wrap his feet up in some old woollen rags.

Unlike the baron's son, the serf's son usually covered his head when he went out. In the winter he wore a shapeless, thick woollen cloak with a wide hood attached to it. At other times he generally wore some kind of bonnet or cap, over which he sometimes tied a wide straw hat, if he wanted to keep the sun out of his eyes.

Poorer girls

A girl in a poor family first put on a shift, and then a long kirtle. They were both equally shapeless, and were made of coarse, unbleached wool. Like their brothers, girls in poor families usually went barefoot, but sometimes they strapped a pair of rough wooden pattens under their feet, to lift them just a little out of the mud.

Materials

Nearly all families in Norman times made their own clothes. Better-off people usually grew enough flax to make all their own linen, and the poor kept a few sheep which

61 Ploughing. Notice the peasants' clothing.

provided wool. It was the women's job to wash, bleach and spin the yarn, and perhaps dye it with some simple vegetable dyes, but it was usually left to the men of the family to weave the yarn into cloth.

62 A woman spins as she feeds the birds.

Even a baron's family normally wore clothes made from local linen and wool. English cloth was so highly esteemed that it had been exported to the Continent for centuries. Occasionally, however, a wealthy family would buy some cloth from another part of England or even from abroad at a fair, if the colour or weave of the material just happened to take their fancy. It would be made up by their servants.

Bed clothes

Most people in Norman times went to bed in their underclothes. But many rich people preferred to wear nothing, and just covered themselves simply with thick blankets and rugs. There are even drawings of kings and queens lying in bed completely naked, except for their crowns, which the artist presumably added to show just how important they were!

11 Games and Festivals

Games

The Normans were renowned as fine warriors, and so it is not surprising that one of the most popular games among boys was known as "miniature combat". The boys were dressed in suits of chainmail and carried lances and shields, but what the rules of the game were (if any!) is not at all clear.

When the weather was too bad to go out, the boys fought with puppets instead. The puppets were usually about 30-40 centimetres high, and looked exactly like

63 Norman fighters — in chainmail, with sword and shield, or with a sling. This is an illustration of David and Goliath.

64 Ball game

65 Children's version of tilting the quintain.

real Norman knights. The game was played by two boys standing or kneeling, facing each other and each with a puppet. The puppets were attached to strings which the boys moved backwards and forwards so that they appeared to fight.

Another very popular sport among older boys was wrestling, and both boys and girls of all ages enjoyed various ball games. One of the most popular was a kind of bowls, and another was hockey or hurling, played with a long curved wooden stick and a small wooden ball.

In the summer children went swimming if they lived near the sea or a river, but they could do only the breast-stroke, as no other stroke had been invented in Norman times. Boys also played a game in the water which was rather like tilting the quintain, except that the boys used a long stick instead of a lance to try to hit the target.

In the winter, of course, children must

66 Bob-apple.

have enjoyed throwing snowballs. They also liked to cut a large lump of ice from the top of a pond and use it to go sledging. Some of the more daring even tied the shin bones from animals to the bottom of their shoes or boots and went skating on the frozen ponds and lakes.

A favourite indoor game in the winter was bob-apple. Children also played a wide variety of games that all involved dice. As a people, the Normans were very fond of gambling, and even the children liked to play a game in which there was the added excitement of being able to bet on the result.

Festivals in the country

For country children one of the most exciting days of the year was Lammas. This was the day when the very first ears of wheat of that year's harvest were cut. A day or so later there was the Loaf Mass, as it was called, when a loaf made from the first ears was taken to the local church to be consecrated and used for communion.

After the harvest was gathered in there was a great harvest supper. In the country the lord of the manor would invite all his workers and their families to join in the feast at his expense. This was the one time of the year when even the poorest people had all the food they could eat (including as much meat as they wanted, since most of the animals had to be slaughtered in the autumn).

In November everyone had to give a hand in gathering in the logs for the winter. Even the children used to help, and the lord of the manor would give the peasants one free log for themselves out of every load they brought home. Later there would be a great feast (at the lord's expense again), and it was also a tradition in most country places that the lord should provide a free bonfire as part of the jollifications.

Christmas

The next great feast in Norman times was, of course, Christmas. This lasted for twelve days, from Christmas Day itself until Epiphany, on 6 January. It was a holiday for everyone, both in the country and in the towns, although naturally some essential jobs, like looking after the animals, still had to be done.

In some churches at Christmas a short nativity play was put on. It was performed by the priests, and took the place of the sermon that was normally given during the course of the mass. This must have been very exciting for the children, as there were no theatres in Norman times, and most of

67   Making a bonfire.

them would probably never have seen any kind of acting before. The first scene of the play usually showed the Annunciation and the Visitation. Then some angels would draw back a curtain to reveal a statue of the Madonna and Child. In the final scene, the shepherds and the three wise men

68 This is a picture from a 12th-century bible of Christ and the disciples on the road to Emmaus. The figures are dressed as 12th-century pilgrims.

would all go up to the statue to lay their gifts reverently at the feet of the Baby King.

69   A dressed and dancing animal.

Easter

At Easter too a short play was performed in some of the churches. It showed the disciples finding the empty tomb, and perhaps Jesus joining them on their walk to Emmaeus. In later Norman times there were similar short plays performed in some churches on all the more important saints' days, which were, of course, always public holidays at that period.

Entertainers

Although there were no theatres there were plenty of wandering entertainers in Norman times. They were always to be seen, for instance, at the great fairs which used to travel all over the country. They included jugglers, acrobats, people playing pipes and drums or perhaps some other instruments, and even people with monkeys and dancing bears.

Wandering entertainers also used to visit the great castles. They were particularly welcome at times like Christmas, or whenever the baron happened to have some important guests. If they were musicians they often played in the minstrels' gallery, which was at one end of the great hall, but other types of entertainers performed in the centre of the hall, in front of the high table.

One type of entertainer who came to the castles was called a jongleur. Our modern word juggler comes from this name, but in fact the average jongleur could do much more than just juggle. He could usually sing, play several musical instruments (such as a lute and a violin) and do acrobatics, as well as tell many amusing anecdotes and tales. The other wandering entertainers who came to the castles were known as troubadours. They usually travelled in small groups, and sang romantic love songs to the accompaniment of a guitar. The troubadours were considered superior to the jongleurs, because they composed all their own material, but they were probably all equally popular with the children in the castles which they visited!

70   A jongleur.

Date List

	Events at Home	Religious Foundations	Events Abroad
1066	William the Conqueror won the Battle of Hastings and was crowned King	Battle Abbey begun	
1068	Saxon rebellion at Exeter		
1069	Saxon rebellion at York (3000 Normans slaughtered) followed by the Waste of the North (the Normans' revenge)		Swein, King of Denmark, sent assistance to the Saxon rebels at York
1070	Lanfranc became Archbishop of Canterbury. Saxon rebellion at Ely, led by Hereward the Wake, which lasted four years		
1071			The Battle of Manzikert, in which Byzantium lost Asia Minor to the Turks
1072		Lincoln Cathedral begun	
1077		Transepts and Nave of St Alban's Cathedral begun	
1079		Transepts of Winchester Cathedral begun	
1083		Ely Cathedral begun	
1086	The Domesday Book compiled		
1087	William the Conqueror died, and was succeeded by his son, William Rufus	Tewkesbury Abbey begun	
1091			The Normans completed their conquest of Sicily
1093	Anselm became Archbishop of Canterbury	The Nave of Durham Cathedral begun	
1095			The First Crusade set out, led by Peter the Hermit

Events at Home	Religious Foundations	Events Abroad
1096	The Nave of Norwich Cathedral begun The Choir of Canterbury Cathedral begun	
1099		The Crusaders established a Christian kingdom at Jerusalem
1100 William Rufus died, and was succeeded by his brother, Henry I		

Glossary

apprentice	someone who was learning a trade or a craft, especially someone who had bound himself to a master craftsman to train for a certain number of years (usually seven)
bailey	the outer courtyard of a castle
baron	in Norman times one of the tenants-in-chief of the King
bower	a lady's private room
clerk	a scholar, frequently employed in Norman times as a copyist or account keeper
cloisters	a covered walk forming part of a monastery or nunnery
cottar	a peasant occupying a cottage on a large estate
Domesday Book	a book compiled on the orders of William the Conqueror, containing an assessment of the population, the land, the stock and so on of the whole of England, for the purposes of taxation
feudal system	the system by which vassals held land from their superiors in return for doing some kind of service for them (especially military service)
flax	a plant with a blue flower, cultivated for the fibre obtained from the stem which was used to make linen
gauntlet	a long glove covering the wrist
great hall	the principal room of a castle
hawking	the sport of hunting birds with hawks especially trained for this purpose
hundred	part of a county, originally occupied by one hundred families
jongleur	a kind of minstrel
journeyman	a skilled craftsman who had completed his apprenticeship
jousting	fighting on horseback with a lance against a mounted opponent similarly armed, often at a tournament

67

keep	the innermost and strongest part of a castle
kirtle	a woman's gown
knight	in Norman times a man bearing a certain military rank, who normally fought on horseback
Lammas	the feast of the first-fruits, on 1 August, sometimes called the loaf-mass festival
lord of the manor	the occupant of a manor house
manor	in Norman times one of the areas of land held by a baron
moat	a deep ditch round a castle, usually filled with water
motte	an artificial mound of earth
patten	a wooden sole or shoe mounted on an iron ring to raise the wearer's feet out of the mud
puttee	a long strip of cloth wound in a spiral pattern round the leg and serving as a gaiter
Quadrivium	a course of study consisting of arithmetic, music, geometry and astrology
quintain	an upright post, at the top of which was a pivoted cross-piece with a board at one end and a sand-bag at the other
reeve	the name given to certain officials who had administrative duties of various kinds
regals	a small portable organ
serf	in Norman times a slave attached to an estate who could be transferred with the estate to a new land-owner at any time
sheriff	a contraction of shire-reeve, an official concerned with maintaining law and order
shire	an area of land, consisting of a number of hundreds, but in Norman times not usually as big as a modern county
sokeman	a sub-tenant
solar	the principal room of a house, constructed if possible to catch the sunshine
steward	an estate manager
tenant-in-chief	someone (usually a baron) holding land directly from the King
tilting	galloping up to a quintain and trying to hit the board at the top with a lance, while at the same time trying to avoid being hit by the sand-bag
tonsure	the shaved crown of a monk's or priest's head
Trivium	a course of study consisting of grammar, rhetoric and logic
troubadour	a writer and singer of romantic poems
villein	a peasant allowed to cultivate a certain number of strips of land for himself in return for working three or more days on his master's land
wattle and daub	a form of wall construction consisting of wooden hurdles covered with plaster

Places to Visit

Alnwick Castle, Northumberland	Keep, armoury and museum
Bamburgh Castle, Northumberland	Great hall and armoury
Battle Abbey, East Sussex	Remains of abbey founded by William the Conqueror
Buildwas Abbey, Shropshire	12th-century abbey, with vaulted chapter house
Cardiff Castle, South Glamorganshire	12th-century keep
Castle Hedingham, Essex	Fine Norman keep
Chepstow Castle, Gwent	11th-13th-century castle
Colchester Castle, Essex	11th-century keep, also museum
Christchurch Castle, Dorset	Ruins of Norman house in the bailey of 11th-century castle
Durham Cathedral, County Durham	Outstanding example of Norman architecture
Fountains Abbey, North Yorkshire	Ruins of 12th-century Cistercian Abbey
Gloucester Cathedral, Gloucestershire	Magnificent Norman building
Hastings Castle, East Sussex	Ruins of Norman castle
Haughmond Abbey, Shropshire	Remains of Augustinian monastery, including chapter house with fine Norman doorway
Kenilworth Castle, Warwickshire	Keep and great hall
London, The Tower	White Tower, chapel and Royal Armouries
London, Victoria and Albert Museum	Large copy of the Bayeux Tapestry (a tapestry depicting life in England at the time of the Conquest)
Orford Castle, Suffolk	Fine Norman keep
Pembroke Castle, Pembrokeshire	Moated Norman castle
Rievaulx Abbey, North Yorkshire	Ruins of magnificent Cistercian abbey
Tewkesbury Abbey, Gloucestershire	Magnificent Norman tower
Winchester Cathedral, Hampshire	Fine Norman architecture
Worcester Cathedral, Worcestershire	Largest Norman crypt in England

Also many more castles, abbeys and churches

Books for Further Reading

Non-Fiction

Ralph Arnold, *A Social History of England, 55BC to 1215 AD* , Constable
Hugh Braun, *The English Castle*, B.T. Batsford
Christopher Brooke, *The Saxon and Norman Kings*, B.T. Batsford
Iris Brooke, *English Costume of the Early Middle Ages*, A. & C. Black
Alfred Duggan, *Growing up with the Norman Conquest,* Faber and Faber
John Finnemore, *Social Life in England, Book I*, A. & C. Black
M. & C.H.B. Quennell, *A History of Everyday Things in England, Vol. I*, B.T. Batsford
O.G. Tomkeieff, *Life in Norman England*, B.T. Batsford

Fiction

Charles Kingsley, *Hereward the Wake*, Blackie
Rosemary Sutcliffe, *Knight's Fee*, Oxford University Press
Rosemary Sutcliffe, *The Shield Ring*, Oxford University Press
Henry Treece, *The Hounds of the King*, The Bodley Head
Henry Treece, *Man with a Sword*, The Bodley Head

Index

The numbers in **bold type** refer to the figure numbers of the illustrations